Original title:
Morning Glory Musings

Copyright © 2025 Creative Arts Management OÜ
All rights reserved.

Author: Gideon Barrett
ISBN HARDBACK: 978-1-80566-784-1
ISBN PAPERBACK: 978-1-80566-804-6

The First Light's Embrace

The sun peeks in, so bright and bold,
My sleepy face, it starts to scold.
The coffee pot gurgles, what a treat,
I trip on slippers, oh what a feat!

The cat stretches wide, like a yoga pro,
Chasing dust bunnies, he steals the show.
Birds tweet nonsense, oh what a choir,
While I look for pants, slightly on fire!

Fresh Beginnings

A rooster crows, it's far too loud,
I wave my pillow, feeling proud.
My cereal dances like it knows the score,
While I debate if I still need to snore.

The sun spills honey on the floor,
I jump around as it starts to pour.
Plants wave back, their leaves all green,
I swear they laugh, it's quite a scene!

Daybreak's Canvas

The sky paints pink, a masterpiece tall,
I drop my toast, watch it take a fall.
Eggs in a scramble, just like my hair,
A dance of chaos fills the air!

Birds start their chatter, a gossip spree,
While I chase my dreams with the last cup of tea.
The sun throws confetti, a bright parade,
And I clumsily join in, work plans delayed!

Awakening Moments

I yawn so wide, like I'm taking flight,
The alarm clock beeps, oh what a fright!
Socks in a tangle, oh what a mess,
I laugh at my wardrobe's boldness and stress.

Outside, the world is buzzing and bright,
I scramble for breakfast, not quite polite.
With one shoe on and the other adrift,
I'm ready to conquer, but wait, just a swift!

Echoes in the Stillness

The rooster crows, a cheeky shout,
While I just stare, still in a pout.
Coffee brews with a splatter sound,
As socks I find all over the ground.

Birds are chirping, quite a band,
Yet here I sit, spoon in hand.
The toast pops up, a little fright,
Perfect start to a clumsy flight.

Hues of the Rising Sun

Orange and pink in the sky collide,
Pajamas on, I choose to hide.
The lawn gnomes seem to grin and wave,
While I contemplate how to misbehave.

A squirrel darts across the path,
Catching sights of my morning wrath.
I trip on shoes left by the door,
Adding to life's great comic lore.

Gentle Touch of Daybreak

The sun peeks in, a bright intruder,
Reminding me I'm far from a hooter.
Kettle whistles, a shrill delight,
I spill it all, oh what a sight!

With cereal flying, I start my race,
Chasing after my favorite lace.
Pancakes flip with a hopeful cheer,
Landing safely, am I in the clear?

Daylight's Embrace

Sunshine kisses my cheek so bold,
While my blanket feels like pure gold.
The dog rolls over, a furry mound,
Next to my heap of laundry found.

I swear I heard a tree branch laugh,
As I tripped over my dog's night bath.
But with a grin and a big ol' sigh,
I embrace the chaos, oh me, oh my!

Embracing the Rising Sun

The rooster crows, it's time to rise,
I trip on shoes, oh what a surprise.
Coffee brews, and toast does pop,
Can't find my keys, I'm ready to flop.

Sunshine peeks through curtains tight,
I dance around in pajamas too bright.
The cat gives me a judging stare,
While I grace the day without a care.

A Prelude to Possibility

A pancake flips with a perfect splat,
As syrup drips down, oh how 'bout that?
The dog steals bacon right off my plate,
Guess this day won't be that great.

Socks don't match—what a fine sight,
I embrace my style—fashion's delight.
The mirror laughs, reflects my grin,
Today's a good day, let the fun begin.

Dancing with Dawn's Embrace

The sun does rise, and so do I,
Trip over slippers, oh my, oh my.
Breakfast waits, it's a chaotic feast,
With cereal flying, I grin at least.

The toast pops up, with a little zing,
My dance moves rival an awkward fling.
A giggle escapes, as I take a bow,
The day is calling, what chaos now?

Serene Moments at Day's Break

Birds are chirping, but I am late,
I trip on the mat—what's my fate?
Coffee on my shirt, it's a fashion trend,
Yet somehow, smiles form—hearts to mend.

The sun's a joker, playing with light,
Mismatched socks, what a silly sight.
I'll strut my stuff in this glorious sun,
With laughter and joy, the day has begun.

Illuminated Thoughts

A rooster strutted, loud and proud,
His wake-up call was like a crowd.
Coffee brews, a bubbling cheer,
Yet here I sit, in PJs, dear.

Sunlight spills, a golden stream,
Chasing away my sleepy dream.
My cat leaps forth, a ninja's charm,
Swatting at dust, with feline calm.

Cascading Rays of Hope

The toast is burnt, a crispy fate,
Yet I still smile, it's never too late.
The newspaper's news, so wild and strange,
Promises today will bring some change.

Out the window, squirrels play tag,
While I sip tea in a cozy rag.
I join the fun but quickly trip,
My laughter flows like a coffee sip.

Dew-kissed Dreams

Dewdrops dance on blades of grass,
As I stumble toward breakfast, alas!
My cereal goes flying high,
Like a bird, I watch it fly by.

The dog runs 'round like he's on fire,
Chasing the sun, his heart's desire.
Frogs play leapfrog, what a prank,
As I spill syrup, oh, how I stank!

Awakening the Soul

A jogger zooms past, oh my grace,
While I trip on lace, what a race!
Birds chime in with their morning chat,
I join their song, but sound like a cat.

With pancakes stacked, I take a bite,
A syrup river, such a delight!
The sun beams down, the day is bright,
With laughter and joy, we take flight.

Reflections in Morning Dew

The sun peeks through the leaves,
A squirrel brushes his hair,
While I sip my coffee,
Trying to hide from the glare.

Grass whispers secrets, you see,
As ants march in a line,
They must have a grand meeting,
Discussing their lunch plans divine.

A cat yawns, takes the throne,
On the fence, proud and spry,
While the birds crack silly jokes,
As if they're ready to fly.

And there I sit, bemused,
In a robe like a cape,
Witnessing life unfold,
In my coffee-stained landscape.

Beneath the Tender Sky

The clouds are having a chat,
Gossiping like old friends,
While I chase down my hat,
In the breeze, the laughter blends.

A dog thinks he's a wolf,
Chasing butterflies with glee,
While a snail takes a selfie,
Slow-mo style, that's the key.

The flowers wear their best dresses,
Showing off their spring flair,
While I trip on my own feet,
And tumble into thin air.

But here under the tender sky,
With petals mixed in my hair,
I'd trade my clumsy moments,
For mischief in the fresh air.

Petals of Promise

The daisies throw a party,
With bees dancing on the side,
While I'm just trying to remember,
Where I put my morning pride.

A butterfly flaps with style,
Wings like a dancing queen,
But trips over a clover,
Making quite a funny scene.

The potted plants are gossiping,
In tiny pots they stay,
While I promise to water them,
But first, I'll nap all day.

Caught in petals of promise,
With giggles in the dew,
I guess tomorrow I'll tend to them,
But today, it's just a view.

The Call of the Yawning Day

The rooster makes a racket,
As if it's got a big plan,
While I roll over to snooze,
In my sleepy, cozy span.

A cup of tea is brewing,
The steam is like a hug,
But the bread in the toaster,
Is taking a warm, toasty slug.

The sun yawns loud and wide,
Stretching over the hills,
While squirrels throw acorns,
And gather their morning thrills.

So here I sit with giggles,
In this comical ballet,
Embracing the silly moments,
In the call of the yawning day.

The Symphony of Daybreak

The rooster crows, a clucky sound,
As sleepy heads spin round and round.
Coffee brews with a happy gurgle,
While socks revolt, they twist and twirl.

The sun peeks in with a cheeky grin,
I swear I hear the light say, 'Let's begin!'
Birds are chirping their morning tune,
But I'm still snuggled, dreaming of noon.

The cereal dances in the bowl,
While cats plot mischief with a stroll.
The toast pops up, a crispy sight,
The morning just loves a friendly fight.

So here we are, the day's new guest,
With laughter first, who needs the rest?
In this wacky, sunny parade,
Why wake up early? Oh, why not? Hooray!

A Canvas of Soft Hues

Brush strokes of orange paint the sky,
While my hair rebels, oh my oh my!
Pajamas cling, they want to stay,
But the sun winks, like, 'Not today!'

A canvas spread in morning light,
The cat does yoga, what a sight!
Socks mismatched, they cause a fuss,
Yet here we are, just laugh with us.

Pancakes flip like acrobats,
One lands on the floor, oh where's the mats?
Syrup drizzles like honey rain,
As I chase crumbs with all my gain.

With paints and giggles, the day rolls on,
The fun is here, until it's gone.
So let's create our morning cheer,
With colors bright, we'll persevere!

Awakening in Sunbeams

Sunbeams tickle my sleepy face,
As I stumble to find my place.
A mismatch of shoes greets the floor,
And my caffeine stash is calling for more.

The dog spins in a wild ballet,
Trying to steal my slice of prey.
While toast is burning, I just grin,
This circus of morning means I win.

The clock is laughing, time's on a spree,
It's 8 AM, oh dear me!
With giggles echoing in this space,
I'll conquer the day at my own pace.

So here's to the dawn, with its funny flight,
Let's jive and dance until it's night.
In sunbeam glories we find our way,
Together we laugh, come what may!

Chasing the First Light

As dawn tiptoes with gentle grace,
I chase the sun like it's a race.
In mismatched socks, I sprint and slide,
With coffee hopes and a hungry guide.

The world sparkles in morning's glow,
While my cat prances, putting on a show.
The toast pops up, with flair and zest,
Breakfast battles, I'm truly blessed.

Butterfly wings in the crisp air swirl,
While my hair's a masterpiece, an artful twirl.
Outside, the laughter of kids unfolds,
Their morning grins, a treasure to hold.

In this chase, we find our fun,
With silly dances under the sun.
So let's embrace this goofy flight,
As we chase the first burst of light!

Echoes of the Early Wind

The rooster sings without a clue,
While I sip coffee, missing my shoe.
The cat's caught a nap in the sunbeam's glow,
Dreaming of mice and a midnight show.

The mailman waves, with a grin so wide,
But I still can't find where my keys decide.
Birds chirp tunes that must be a plot,
To steal my breakfast, or maybe not.

A neighbor's dog starts a woeful tune,
Competing with squirrels for a piece of the moon.
I chuckle softly, this chaos I love,
As ants march by in their little white gloves.

A pancake flips, oh what a surprise,
And lands right on my neighbor's prize.
In laughter we share, at the antics of day,
The morning brings giggles, so come what may.

The Lightness of Being

I tripped on a banana while trying to dance,
My dog thought it'd give him a chance.
He leaped with grace across the room,
And knocked over my plant - oh, what a boom!

Sunshine tickles the window blinds,
As I search for my socks, two different kinds.
A squirrel peeks in, it's quite the sight,
I swear he's plotting my hilarious plight.

Cereal's dancing, and milk jumps too,
My bowl's a circus, oh yes, it's true.
A spoon flies out like it wants to flee,
While I giggle back at the wild morning spree.

The toaster pops, but not the bread,
Just a crumb that flew straight at my head.
With laughter I ponder this ruckus that sprung,
Is life just a song that's constantly sung?

Dawn's Quiet Revelations

The sun cracks a smile on my sleepy face,
As I stumble about in a warm, fuzzy race.
The cat's on the counter, no concept of time,
And I'm just a jester in this morning rhyme.

Coffee machine gurgles, a strange little beast,
While pigeons outside hold a noisy feast.
Did I hear a giggle? Oh dear, it was me,
Chasing the dreams that were fresh as can be.

The toast pops up, but it's too late,
I've already burned my last slice of fate.
A butterfly lands on my milk jug's rim,
Is it judging my breakfast? It's making me grim.

Yet laughter erupts like the sun through the trees,
As I chase that butterfly, all wobbly knees.
In the madness of dawn, with its quirky grace,
I find the fun in the sleepy race.

The Beauty of the Unseen

A sock on the ceiling, what a strange sight,
I'd blame the cat, but he's snug and tight.
The ceiling fan spins with a wild, crazy glow,
Why does it tickle, and who really knows?

I'm tangled in sheets like a subdued burrito,
A gardener woefully pruning a potato.
Laughter erupts from an unseen guest,
Who's gloating over this early morning jest.

My breakfast sneezed, or so it seemed,
As the toast offered up crumbs - oh how it dreamed!
The orange juice giggles, it's almost alive,
Turning my day into a carnival dive.

I step on a Lego, oh what a luck,
And laugh at my luck, feeling quite struck.
The beauty of chaos spins wildly around,
In the unseen laughter, pure joy can be found.

Day's First Kiss

The rooster crows, a morning tune,
I swear he's singing just for the moon.
Coffee brews like magic's spell,
Hoping it wakes me from this shell.

Butterflies dance, or maybe flies,
Crashing into window with loud sighs.
Pajamas clinging, I'm up with flair,
Wondering if I should comb my hair.

Toast pops up, a golden cheer,
It's the breakfast champion of the year.
With jelly spreading, it's a delight,
Who knew mornings could feel so bright?

The cat yawns wide with a snooty glance,
As if he's judging my morning dance.
But I'll embrace the day with glee,
Let laughter rule, oh, let it be!

Radiant Horizons

Sunrise creeps in with a bright pink grin,
Time to wake up, let the day begin.
Birds are chirping their cheeky song,
It's a concert start, can't be wrong!

Socks don't match, but I don't care,
Fashion statements float in the air.
Breakfast scattered, a culinary mess,
Still, I feel like I'm truly blessed.

Neighbors peek out, coffee in hand,
Now we're a sitcom—oh, isn't it grand?
We share our quirks with laughter too loud,
Here's to mornings, we're merry and proud!

"Did you see that squirrel?" someone yells,
As it dances through our breakfast bells.
This is our stage, every sunrise new,
Let's make it funny, me, and you!

Whispered Wishes at Sunrise

Mornings wink with a playful tease,
Whispers of daylight drift on a breeze.
I trip on my shoelace, oh what a bother,
Maybe I'll get a dog instead of a father.

Java in hand, I fight the yawn,
Recalling the dreams that quietly shone.
A croissant flies out like a bird in flight,
Breakfast seems ready for a light-hearted fight.

Sunshine splashes over messy hair,
I'd trade my brush for a magic flair.
Today's agenda: giggles and plays,
Let's embrace the silly in all of our ways.

"Is that a unicorn?" someone declares,
No, just my laundry's colorful snares!
Even in chaos, laughter's the prize,
Morning's sweet kiss is a grand surprise!

Threads of New Light

A tapestry woven with daybreak threads,
Cats and creatures jumping out of beds.
Sunlight tickles our sleepy faces,
Ticking away all the tired places.

My toast does a flip, a daredevil try,
Lands butter-side down—what a sly guy!
The mailbox stands like a fortress old,
Filled with bills but never with gold.

Neighbors erupt in a loud good cheer,
At the sound of a sneeze, the joke is clear.
"Mornings are hilarious when laughter's the goal,
Let's welcome today with a silly stroll!"

Chasing the shadows, we giggle away,
Life is too precious for serious play.
So let's dance on the grass and embrace the round,
For in these bright moments, true joy is found!

Golden Hues of Hope

Sunshine spills like milk on toast,
Birds chirp gossip, bragging host.
Socks mismatched, a colorful fight,
Coffee spills, adding to delight.

Butterflies dance with a silly grace,
Chasing shadows in a bright race.
Toast jumps, pops, looks quite surprised,
Breakfast antics, all well advised.

Laughter bubbles with every cup,
Sipping joy while cats cheer up.
Playful thoughts swirl in the air,
Tomorrow's dreams still in our hair.

Fresh Morning Promises

Roosters crowing with morning flair,
Neighbors mumble, half unaware.
Joggers trip on their own two feet,
While coffee thieves claim victory sweet.

A dog runs wild, chasing its tail,
As pigeons plot their sneaky fail.
The sun peeks in, a mischievous grin,
Time to see what fun's about to begin!

Jams on toast, they dance like fools,
Honey spills while we share our jewels.
Laughs erupt over silly quotes,
Life's a ride in comical boats.

Echoes of New Beginnings

Alarm clocks beep like angry bees,
Jumping out of dreams with ease.
Mismatched socks on the floor take flight,
Tickle and tease with morning's height.

Cereal sings as it splashes down,
Milk floods the bowl, like a clumsy clown.
Pajamas still on, what's the rush?
Life's a whirlwind, let's not crush.

Necklaces made of spaghetti strings,
Dancing with joy, oh, the joy it brings!
Breakfast is chaos, yet so divine,
New adventures await us to dine.

A Palette of Possibilities

Paint the morning with silly schemes,
Wake up dreaming colorful dreams.
Muffins hop from the oven high,
Lap it up, kids, oh me, oh my!

Pancakes flip with a wink and a shout,
A syrup river flowing without doubt.
A cat plays tag with a flying spoon,
Life's a carnival under the moon!

Sunshine tickles the sleepy face,
Each new hour, we set the pace.
Laughter soars on a golden breeze,
Every moment's a dance with ease.

Dawn's Gentle Whisper

The sun peeks in with a cheeky grin,
While my cat yells, 'Where have you been?'
Coffee brews with a playful hiss,
As I dream of an early morning bliss.

Birds are chirping their silly tunes,
They're strutting like they own the moons.
I trip on shoes all tangled in plight,
Yet I welcome the day, oh what a sight!

Pancakes flip with a joyful flop,
Eggs doing salsa, I can't make them stop.
In my head, a parade of cheer,
Every sunrise feels like a carnival here.

So here's to laughter with every dawn,
With sleepy smiles and a funny yawn.
Let's embrace this light, what a delight,
In the zany world of morning's bite.

Awakening Light

The rooster crows in a playful way,
I stumble down like a disarray.
Breakfast waits, but the toast's on strike,
As the butter melts with a sassy spike.

My socks don't match, they dance in glee,
One is blue, the other, a kiwi.
The cereal sings a crunchy song,
While the milk does a wobbly prong.

Plants poke out their leaves with sass,
Waving to the neighbors, all in mass.
Clouds drift by like a cotton ball,
As I try to catch them, but I fall.

Shiny sun beams down with a wink,
I sip my coffee and start to think.
Today's the day I'll strive for light,
In this quirky world, everything feels right!

Radiance of New Beginnings

With a yawn that could wake the dead,
I fumble for my glasses instead.
The toast pops up like a jack in the box,
Sizzling and crackling, oh what a hoax!

My shoes were hiding under the bed,
Laughing, they say, 'Just wake up, Fred!'
The clock is laughing, it's nearly late,
But here's the fun—let's tempt fate!

Lemonade spills on my favorite shirt,
I yell, 'It's a fashion statement, not dirt!'
The sun shines bright, but so is my hair,
A wild nest—but who would care?

Let's dance in the kitchen, take a twirl,
With slippers that spin and jump and whirl.
Today's a canvas, so colorful and wide,
With joyful chaos as my guide!

Sunlit Dreams Unfold

Under blankets, I fight like a knight,
'Just five more minutes' feels so right.
The sun blasts in, takes off my sheets,
And laughs as I grumble with puffy feet.

Oatmeal's bubbling, a creamy affair,
But the spoon has vanished—whoops, where's the pair?
Cats have plotted, they plan their raids,
While I scold them in my pajama spades.

Windows flicker with sparkling cheer,
Who needs coffee when chaos is near?
The furniture's dancing as I walk by,
And even the fridge lets out a sigh.

So let's find joy in this playful scene,
With laughter that bubbles, bright and serene.
Each playful moment a treasure to keep,
As the day unfolds, my heart takes a leap.

Radiant Reflections

I woke up too late, oh what a sight,
My hair's a nest, a bird took flight.
Coffee's brewing, I spilled the grounds,
Mirror laughs, with silly sounds.

Sunlight spills like syrup sweet,
Dodging shadows, I trip on my feet.
Pajamas waving, a fashion faux pas,
But hey, it's home, so who cares, ya?

The toast pops up, a joyful cheer,
Burnt on one side, but never fear.
Jams and jellies, they dance on bread,
While I wonder what's inside my head.

So raise a mug to this wild start,
With laughter and joy that fills the heart.
Life's too short for morning strife,
Let's embrace the chaos, love this life!

Whispering Petals at Dawn

The flowers giggle, they're in their bloom,
As I stumble 'round, bringing the gloom.
Bees buzzing near, what a loud affair,
I offer them sugar, they just stare.

The sun peeks out, plays hide and seek,
While my cat plots mischief, that rascal sneak.
Pollen sneezes make for a cheeky tune,
As the morning yawns, a little cartoon.

Birds tweet their news, a lively chat,
While I chase them off with a flapping hat.
Nature's gossip, a blissful mess,
Who knew that sunrise could be so blessed?

So let's prance among the petals bright,
With whispers of laughter in morning light.
We might trip and fall, oh what a sight,
But I'll rise again with all my might.

Chasing the Golden Hour

Alarm clock screams, what a rude surprise,
I snort awake, rubbing my eyes.
The golden hour's slipping away,
As I fumble for clothes, what a clumsy ballet.

Coffee spills while I dance on toes,
Lips stained brown from yesterday's woes.
Is that a muffin or a rock?
I'll find out soon, just give it a knock.

The toast does a flip; it's quite the sight,
Landing butter-side down, oh what a fright!
But laughter erupts with every mishap,
As I embrace the morning in style and cap.

So here I am, in my mismatched flair,
With a goofy grin, I've lost my care.
Chasing that glow till it fades from view,
In this wacky morning, I'm feeling brand new!

The Dance of Early Light

In the early light, my sock feels lumpy,
I check twice, what's found is quite jumpy.
Did my laundry turn into an art show?
With polka dots flying, it's quite the tableau.

The sun stretches wide, yawning with glee,
As I trip on the mat, oh woe is me!
The coffee pot bubbles, a symphony loud,
While I wave around like I'm in a crowd.

Breakfast is chaos, ingredients fly,
Eggs land on my head, oh my, oh my!
With a spatula twirl, and an apron askew,
I make a grand feast, just me and my stew.

So dance through the morning, let laughter ignite,
With mishaps and giggles, everything's light.
No stage too small for this daily delight,
Let's celebrate life, in its pure, silly light!

Dawn's Soft Revelations

A rooster crows, but not in tune,
He missed his shot, can he sing at noon?
The sun peeks in, a lazy grin,
While sleepy heads just want to sin.

Coffee brews with anxious sighs,
Dancing grounds, my morning prize.
Toast pops up like a jack-in-box,
Butter spins like disco clocks.

Cats prance around, a cereal raid,
Tiptoeing, they'll never get paid.
Chasing sunlight, they leap and bound,
As if the world's a playground found.

But wait, what's that? A sock on the floor,
Who needs a match? Just wear two more!
In this soft light, absurdity reigns,
Let's tackle this day—with laughter's gains!

Enchantment in the Early Light

The sun winks at the moon's retreat,
As the alarm goes off, that stubborn cheat.
Bouncing out of bed, what's the plan?
Still wearing yesterday's jammy span.

The cat looks on; I think she smirks,
As I stumble through my morning quirks.
Cereal spills like magical dust,
Why can't I find just one spoon I trust?

Clouds gather round like curious kids,
While I juggle coffee, toast, and lids.
Birds squawk outside in wild debate,
Are they voting on my breakfast fate?

Oh look! My shoe looks like a cat!
Can it walk? Maybe dance? How about that?
In early light, hilarity grows,
Unfolding day, where whimsy flows!

Breaking of the Day

A beeping sound breaks my reverie sweet,
Who decided mornings need this beat?
I hit the snooze with a warrior's grace,
Fighting off sleep like a slow-paced race.

The sun spills in like spilled grape juice,
My eyes squint, begging for a truce.
Oatmeal's bubbling like a witch's brew,
Will it behave? I haven't a clue!

Birds engage in a morning chatter,
Are they gossiping or simply in splatter?
The neighbor's lawn gnome holds his ground,
As I search for my left shoe, still not found.

Why does breakfast come with such fuss?
Yogurt erupts like it's in a rush.
But in the chaos, laughter will stay,
As another silly dawn breaks at play!

The Unfolding Day

The curtains part like a superhero's cape,
Heroes of morning, no time to escape!
I try to stretch like a cat in plight,
But land on my face—oh what a sight!

Pancakes flip with their dramatic flair,
Landing in places; do they even care?
Socks mismatched in an artful way,
Who needs a stylist? I own this display!

The toaster pops like it's made of spring,
Why do we trust this electric thing?
Meanwhile the dog, in a blissful haze,
Snores louder than my morning malaise.

Life unfolds in its quirky way,
With every new dawn, a fresh bouquet.
In laughter and chaos, let's find our way,
To cherish today, come what may!

Awakening Horizons

The rooster crows, a sleep decree,
Coffee spills, oh woe is me!
Socks on wrong, I trip and sway,
The dawn of chaos starts the day.

Toast pops up, black as night,
But I still grin, it feels so right.
With hair like hay, I strut outside,
Embracing morning's wild ride.

Cats stretch wide, then chase a toe,
I laugh so hard, it steals the show.
The garden blooms, a sight most bright,
While I fend off bees in flight.

So here's to mornings, bits of fun,
Where laughter reigns before we run.
With silly moments setting the tone,
Each dawn brings joy, and I'm not alone.

Serenade of the Sun

The sun peeks in, oh what a tease,
As my alarm clock plays the freeze.
Pajamas on, a sight so grand,
I dance like no one's in this land.

Coffee's brewing, oh what a smell,
Like magic beans from wishes well.
I trip on toys, my morning spree,
Dodging pets like they're a spree.

Birds are chirping a comic song,
I join their tune, I can't go wrong.
With mismatched socks and a eager grin,
The day's adventure, let's begin!

So here's to mornings, wild and free,
Each giggle shared, just you and me.
With sunlight's kiss, our worries fade,
Laughter echoes in morning's parade.

Glimmering Possibilities

Waking up with bedhead flair,
I stumble forth, a sleepy bear.
Cereal spills, a crunchy mess,
But who can care? I'm dressed to impress!

A mirror shows my sleepy eyes,
I dub my look 'the avant-garde prize.'
With mismatched outfits and bright, bold hues,
I'm a walking palette of morning muse.

The sun pops out, a playful grin,
Time for adventures to begin.
Plants beg for water, but I just wave,
As I contemplate the joys I crave.

So grab your snack and wear your smile,
Let's take a breather, sit for a while.
Each beat of laughter, possibilities tease,
In this bright day, we're sure to seize.

Aroma of Dawn's Awakening

The scent of toast wafts through the air,
As I trip over my chair, a legendary affair.
The sunbeams giggle on the floor,
A kitten naps, but I want more!

Chirping birds sing their silly rhyme,
While I attempt to sweep in time.
Socks are missing, but do I care?
I'll prance around like a breath of air!

Coffee's bubbling, a frothy brew,
My groggy brain says 'not for you!'
But laughter bubbles, conquering the haze,
As I embrace the craziness of these days.

So let's toast to mornings, full of cheer,
A wacky ride that we hold dear.
With joy and laughter, the sun we'll greet,
In our expedition, there's nothing we can't beat!

A Tapestry of Light

The sun creeps up with a grin,
Birds shout loud, let the day begin.
Coffee pots dance a little jig,
While sleepy cats hold on, so big.

The toast pops up, what a surprise,
Butter jumps, it's time to rise!
Socks go missing, oh what a plight,
The day's cartoonish, oh what a sight!

Sunflowers nod, gossiping leaves,
A squirrel sneaks past in old blue sleeves.
Nature chuckles, unfolds a scheme,
The world awakens, it's all a dream!

With giggles of dew on a leafy throne,
Every stem feels less alone.
With a wink, the breeze takes flight,
In this dance, everything feels right.

Heartbeats of Dawn

A rooster crows, he's quite the show,
Chasing dreams like it's an ego throw.
The world stirs slowly from its night,
While shadows stretch, embracing light.

Pancake batter bubbles with glee,
Flipping those cakes is quite a spree.
Grandpa's snoring, three houses down,
Even the dog wears a sleepy frown.

The mailman trips over a stray cat,
As the flowers giggle, "What's up with that?"
Dewdrops tumble, trying to escape,
Nature's hilarity in every shape.

With every laugh in the day's unlock,
Trees sway gently, check their clock.
The sun rolls in, it's time to play,
In this cheerful, bright array.

Nature's Quiet Epiphany

The grass tickles toes, oh what a feel,
Dirt smiles back with a delightful squeal.
Clouds are laughing, pink with delight,
As butterflies play tag, what a sight!

Rain's soft patter starts a laugh,
Dancing drops on a leafy path.
Squirrels chatter, plotting a heist,
While flowers boast of who's the nicest.

The sun beams down, a golden hug,
While ants march in with a tiny shrug.
A snail's slow-mo, quite the scene,
Throwing shade like a leafy queen.

Laughter echoes in every nook,
Creating flutters like a well-worn book.
Nature whispers in giggles clear,
A genius at play, so simple and dear.

Glimpse of New Horizons

The rooster's fashionably late today,
While breakfast sizzles, hip-hop ballet.
A dog in pajamas runs after a cat,
Not quite a race, but just a chat.

Waking trees spread their arms real wide,
Sluggish squirrels on an acorn ride.
The sun peeks in, a golden eye,
As flowers chuckle and droop nearby.

Each new bloom dons a zany hat,
"Join the party!" they shout with a pat.
A butterfly flutters, showing her flair,
While birds chirp a tune, "Just stop and stare!"

The sky paints stories, doodles and swirls,
As bees gather gossip from pretty girls.
In this laughter of life, we find our grace,
A joyous canvas, a smiling space.

Breath of a New Day

The rooster crows, what a sound,
My snooze button feels so profound.
Coffee calls, a warm embrace,
But the cat steals my favorite space.

Outside, the world is in a spin,
A squirrel steals my breakfast bin.
With toast in hand, I start to dance,
While my dog gives me a sideways glance.

Beneath the Awakened Sky

The clouds above are fluffy and bright,
I'm still tangled in sheets, oh what a sight!
Joggers rush, like ants in a line,
While I contemplate breakfast, and maybe some wine.

Birds are chirping a tune so strange,
I wonder if they're also deranged.
I sip my juice, a little bit spilt,
Oh well, another nuisance built!

Serenity in Sunrise

Sunlight creeps through the window's frame,
Wait, is that my alarm? Nope, wrong name!
Pancakes sizzling on the stove,
If only it came to shove!

The cat jumps high, land with a thud,
While I dream of muffins, wrapped in a fud.
Butterflies flit, bugs slimy in sight,
I think I'll just stay inside, out of fright.

Momentary Glimmers

The morning sun peeks with a grin,
I spill my cereal, oh where to begin?
A dog with a sock looks quite amused,
As I slip and slide, utterly confused.

A neighbor waves, I raise my mug,
Caffeine levels rise, I start to shrug.
The day unfolds, in laughter and play,
Glimmers of fun in my clumsy ballet.

Buds of Possibility

As sunlight spills from the sky,
The flowers giggle, oh my!
Each petal a whisper, a wink,
Nature's joke, don't you think?

Bees buzzing like tiny cars,
Chasing dreams, just like stars.
Squirrels dance, oh what a sight,
Buds of mischief, what's their plight?

The grass yawns and stretches wide,
A tiny worm, the morning's guide.
He wriggles with glee, full of cheer,
Wondering why the day is here.

In this garden, let's explore,
The funny secrets nature bore.
With every bloom, a tale to tell,
Of laughter shared beneath the bell.

Lullabies of the Dawn

A rooster crows a silly tune,
Mice in slippers dance to the moon.
The sun peeks in, all bright and bold,
Whispers of stories yet untold.

A cat sneezes, complaints arise,
As birds chirp back, to tease the skies.
They chatter like it's all a game,
While doggy dreams take on new names.

Fluffy clouds drift like cotton candy,
The world awakens, bright and dandy.
A squirrel shares his breakfast cheer,
While chasing shadows far and near.

In this silly dawn parade,
Where no one seems to be afraid.
Each giggle dances on the breeze,
Ecstatic blooms beneath the trees.

Celestial Canvas of Color

The sun spills paint on the morning floor,
A canvas bright, who could ask for more?
Clouds blush pink, as if they know,
Their day job's just to put on a show.

The bugs wear hats, quite fancy indeed,
While flowers gossip, oh what a breed!
Dancing buds, with styles to flaunt,
In whispers soft, they teasingly taunt.

Butterflies flutter with flair so grand,
Each flutter a joke planned and unplanned.
They twist and twirl, on their way to class,
While ladybugs giggle as they pass.

Nature's palette, pure delight,
A laughing dream, morning so bright.
Each dawn, like laughter, never grows old,
In colors bold, new tales unfold.

The Rise of Radiance

The sun jumps up, a comical sight,
Waking the world with a beam of light.
Trees wave hello, dressed in green,
While critters cheer, a lively scene.

Chickens dance, wings in the air,
Gathering giggles without a care.
The breeze winks, whispers of fun,
And points to the sky where clouds run.

A squirrel teases with acorn tricks,
While mice are plotting their morning mix.
Each creature shares their own delight,
In the rise of radiance, morning bright.

With every chuckle, the day's begun,
Laughter spreads, oh what fun!
The world awaits, come join the spree,
For every dawn is a funny jubilee.

Skylines Painted in Pastels

Sunrise spills colors, oh what a scene,
Birds chirp a tune, like a kid with a dream.
Coffee brews louder than a marching band,
While I find my socks, scattered by hand.

The sun yawns awake, stretching its rays,
I trip on my slippers, caught in a daze.
The neighbor's lawn gnome gives me a wink,
As I dance with my broom, oh don't you think?

Petunias in pots wear hats made of dew,
And bees in their bowties buzz out "How do you?"
Nature's got style, it's quite the parade,
While I slip on a pancake, now I'm afraid!

So here's to the mornings, with all of their quirks,
They come with their laughter, and giggles that lurk.
Let's paint all the skylines in colors so bold,
And dance with our grumpies until we are old.

A Breath of Fresh Seeds

I woke up this morning, my nose all a-twitch,
The weeds in the garden were throwing a pitch.
Pollen and flowers are out on parade,
While sneezing and laughing, I feel quite unmade.

The cat on the windowsill looks quite bemused,
Staring at raindrops, thoroughly confused.
I toss him a treat, he gives me a glare,
As if he'd prefer to fly through the air.

Eggs are a-hollering, frying with flair,
While toast has been plotting a crispy affair.
I spill my juice, oh what a delight,
Splashing on breakfast, like a morning fight.

But fresh seeds of laughter bloom in my heart,
As I flip through the chaos, a true work of art.
So let's plant these moments, with giggles and glee,
And grow us a garden, just you wait and see!

The Essence of Awakening

The rooster yells louder than my own clock,
As I stumble from dreams, in my mismatched sock.
Coffee beans jitter, waiting their turn,
While I debate if I'll let my hair burn.

Sunbeams peek in, like they own the place,
They tickle my nose, what a cheeky embrace.
I swear they're just waiting for me to fall,
But I trip on my shoelaces, fate has a ball.

The toast jumps with pride, a buttery show,
While the spatula dances with skills from below.
The fridge hums a tune, conducting a beat,
As I chaotically juggle my cup and my seat.

Yet amidst all this ruckus, there's joy in the air,
The essence of waking, with love and with care.
So here's to the mess, to the giggles and fumbles,
In the bright of the morn, it's perfectly humble.

The Savor of Stillness

Before the world hums, there's a whispering pause,
A moment of stillness, to tease and to draw.
The clock ticks slowly, like a lazy cat,
While I ponder my dreams, where they wander and spat.

A mug in my hands, warmth hugs my soul tight,
As I sip in the silence, what a wondrous sight.
Birds in the trees argue over their feast,
While I sit and giggle, they're stubborn, at least!

The sun shows its face, in a joyful surprise,
While yawning and stretching, it opens its eyes.
The breeze in the branches hums a soft tune,
And I join in the laughter of morning's commune.

So here's to the stillness, the quiet delight,
The savor of moments, before the mad flight.
Let's relish these snippets, a goofy embrace,
As we plunge into daydreams, at our own quick pace!

Twilight's Last Sigh

The sun is slow to rise and shine,
My coffee's cold, and that's just fine.
Birds are laughing at my bedhead,
I swear, they think I'm still half-dead.

The pets are plotting their escape,
As I attempt to find my cape.
Their antics leave me in a haze,
Just another start to my funny days.

Sunrises and Sorrows

The rooster crows, it's quite absurd,
He's got a joke I haven't heard.
My slippers mocked my sleepy feet,
As I shuffled off for sips of heat.

The toast pops up, a little burnt,
Wishing less 'crunch' was my concern.
And as I face the grinning morn,
I laugh, for sleep is clearly worn.

Threads of Gilded Dawn

Cracks of light through curtains peep,
They mock my dreams, and me, they keep.
A squirrel stunts upon my roof,
I'm starting to question his goof-proof.

The sun's a prankster, it pings my nose,
I hide in shades, but still it glows.
As shadows dance upon my wall,
I know, too well, I'm having a brawl.

Awakening Bliss

The alarms ring, a band in my head,
Can't they see I'd rather stay in bed?
My clothes are missing, where'd they flee?
A wardrobe thief is playing with me!

The cereal boxes mock with glee,
As I chase the milk like a wild bee.
Caught in the whirl of morning's charm,
I laugh and wave it all with calm.

Radiance Unfurled

The sun peeks in, a cheeky grin,
My coffee's cold, let the day begin!
I trip on socks, my breakfast flies,
Dreams of pancakes, oh how they rise!

Birds are chirping, they sound a tune,
While I'm still adjusting to noon.
A squirrel steals toast from the railing,
My very own food-tale, quite derailing!

Sunlit Thoughts

A rooster sings, but oh, what a croak,
Chasing my slippers, it's no idle joke.
Cereal's dancing in the bowl,
While my cat eyes it, with a sly patrol.

The sun spills laughter on the floor,
I trip over pillows, then bounce for more.
Today's agenda: blissful play,
Guess I'll consider work… some other day!

Dreamscapes of the Dawn

Woke up dreaming of a dragon's flight,
But tripped on my dream, just my luck tonight.
My socks clash wildly, a fashion disgrace,
But who needs style with a smile on the face?

Sunbeams giggle as they light the way,
My old cat plans a nap, in splendid array.
I dance with shadows, we spin and twirl,
In my quirky kingdom, it's a wild swirl!

Whispers of the Awakening Sky

Pancakes flip, oh what a mess,
Maple syrup's now in distress.
The dog snickers at my odd ballet,
While I juggle breakfast, come what may.

The sky blushes as I sip and sip,
Ducklings waddle, on their tiny trip.
With giggles and grins, the world seems bright,
Chaos and joy, what a wonderful sight!

The Poetry of Soft Awakening.

The sun peeks in with a glittering grin,
Cats stretch like yoga pros, ready to spin.
Coffee brews with a gurgling cheer,
While toast starts dancing, oh my, oh dear!

The alarm clock shouts with a raspy song,
But the duvet whispers, "Stay here, it's wrong!"
Pajamas are worn like crowns of the day,
In this kingdom of breakfast, we rule and we play!

Socks find their mates in a sock drawer fight,
Where wadded-up pairs seem to rule the night.
Oh, look at the pancakes, they're doing a flip,
While syrup cascades like it's ready to drip!

The sun yawns big, stretching out the sky,
And I join the revelry with a sleepy sigh.
So let's stumble boldly into the bright,
In a world full of giggles, we'll take flight!

Dawn's Gentle Whisper

The rooster crows, but oh, what a sound,
As sleepyheads crawl from dreams, all around.
A mishmash of hair is what we all sport,
As we shuffle toward breakfast, our favorite sort!

Birds tweet gossip, sharing the news,
While coffee pots bubble like they've got the blues.
The newspaper crinkles, a throne made of ink,
While cereals clatter with a wobbly clink!

Sunbeams paint the walls in colors anew,
While socks take a stroll and they're not matching too.
Oh, the joy of a mess waiting just to be seen,
In the castle of morning, where fun reigns supreme!

So here's to the giggles and wobbly cheer,
As we waltz into daylight, let's make it clear:
This day is a canvas, a laugh and a play,
With dawn as our partner, let's dance all the way!

Sunlit Dreams Awaken

The sun bursts forth, a joker in time,
Tickling the shadows, in rhythm and rhyme.
A sleepyhead stretches, yawns like a bear,
As slippers jump off with a spring in the air!

Breakfast is brewing, it's a circus of fun,
With eggs doing flips and toast on the run.
The milk's on a mission, it spills in a dance,
While bacon does the twist, given half a chance!

The clock is a trickster, it jumps all around,
But we're lost in the laughter, no matter the sound.
The cat chases sunlight like it's a game,
As we giggle together, with breakfast the fame!

So let's drink in the cheer like it's fresh squeezed joy,
Embrace all the chaos and antics deployed,
For today is a treasure, a gift wrapped in light,
Let's waddle through fun, in the morning delight!

A Symphony of Sunbeams

Sunbeams tumble like clowns on parade,
Filling the room with a bright serenade.
Blankets toss in laughter, it's time to arise,
With giggles of daylight that quirkily surprise!

A cereal orchestra plays in a bowl,
While spoons tap out rhythms, they play their role.
The milk splashes down for a grand finale,
While the cat moonwalks like it's dancing a rally!

Shoes on the floor have a love-hate affair,
They hide and they seek, forgotten with flair.
But here comes the jam, toast pops up proud,
And breakfast is served to an imaginary crowd!

So let's twirl in the morning, with aprons aligned,
And sip on our drinks where the laughter is kind.
With a symphony playing, we bask in this scene,
Our lives are the music, and we reign supreme!

Glorious Illumination

The sun peeks in with a cheeky grin,
My coffee's strong, let the day begin.
Ollie the cat leaps, a daring stunt,
And I spill my drink—oh, what a front!

Toast in the toaster, it pops with a dance,
Butter slides off like it's in a trance.
The dog snores deep, dreaming of a chase,
While I'm stuck here, stained in pancake grace.

Birds chirp loudly, a raucous choir,
I swear they sing of my newfound attire.
The socks mismatched, one blue, one green,
I'm starting to feel like a coffee bean.

The world awakens, with a laugh and a yell,
Every moment feels like a carnival bell.
So here's to the chaos that mornings do bring,
In the circus of life, we all dance and sing!

Nature's Morning Serenade

The rooster crows, a trumpeting fool,
While squirrels debate who rules the old school.
The flowers giggle, waving their heads,
As I stumble past, coffee brings on my dreads.

A chipmunk scurries, a nut in its cheek,
Is that a treasure, or just a technique?
The sun, a spotlight, warms up the stage,
While the wind plays a tune that's all the rage.

In the garden, a frog jumps, tries a leap,
Lands in the pond—a splash, and a peep!
Nature's symphony is bugling loud,
Meanwhile, I'm grumbling, a sleepy cloud.

So here in this circus, a joyful parade,
Each critter a player, in antics displayed.
With laughter and quirks in this morning play,
A perfect start to the wacky day!

A Dawn's Epiphany

The alarm clock sings, but it's off-key,
I hit snooze once more, just let me be!
The sun's a tease, peeking under the sheet,
While dreams of cupcakes dance on my feet.

In the kitchen, my plan's turning to mush,
Eggs are a scramble, my head in a rush.
Flour flies high like a snowstorm in June,
And my breakfast looks like a cartoonish tune.

The mailbox winks, with bills on parade,
I swear that they know of the trades I once made.
While the neighbors prod, they nod and they grin,
As I fumble my way with an egg on my chin.

Maybe one day I'll wake up with grace,
And tackle the morning, a competent race.
But for now, I'll laugh, accept my dismay,
In the jumbled mess of a blissful day!

Pondering the Dawn

As sunlight spills on sleepy town,
Frogs croak loud, in sleepy frown.
I sip my coffee, spill a bit,
The dog just stares, like he's calling it.

Birds are chirping, what a racket,
Socks on my feet—oh, what a bracket!
To chase the cat or grab the toast,
I think I'll just indulge; I like this most.

The mailman waves, forgets my name,
A morning game, it's all the same.
With birds and dogs, we gather near,
In our little chaos, there's nothing to fear.

Sun climbs high, the rooster crows,
Waking up, my brain still slow.
Life's a joke, just a marching band,
Let's raise a toast with bread in hand!

Daybreak Reflections

Cracked my egg, it danced in the pan,
Like a morning artist, oh what a plan!
Coffee whispers sweet, "Just one more sip,"
But my cup's empty, I'm losing my grip.

The cat stalks sunbeams on the floor,
Imagining battles 'gainst ghosts of yore.
I chuckle aloud, as he takes a dive,
My morning mission? To just survive!

The toast pops up with a startled face,
Screaming, "Eat me!" with perfect grace.
As I napkin-stuff my morning feast,
I spot the neighbor, a lumbering beast.

The day begins with laughter loud,
An ode to joy, I'll make a crowd.
Life's quirky dance under dawning light,
As mornings break, we'll be alright!

The Quiet Promise

The sun peeks out, a timid grin,
Cats are playing the violin.
I trip on slippers, stumble outside,
A bush gave chase, I nearly cried.

Muffin crumbs and butter flies,
Chasing shadows under brightening skies.
The world awakens, a curious spree,
The neighbor's dog stares, is he judging me?

With a smile I wave, then drop my toast,
Mornings like this, I love the most.
Pancakes stack high like a lopsided dream,
Oh, how life bubbles, like whipped up cream!

A quiet promise of laughter ahead,
With golden sunlight, let worries shed.
Embrace the tangle of this day anew,
With goofy delight, let's see this through!

Rhapsody of Rising Light

Birds lead symphonies on rooftops high,
While I juggle breakfast and the drizzle sky.
Omelets flop like my favorite tune,
What's for dinner? Oh wait, it's noon!

The sunbeams twirl like dancers bright,
And I'm just here, trying not to fright.
With mismatched socks and a belt askew,
Dressing up is such hard work, who knew?

Tea's in the kettle, it whistled its song,
And the clock ticks fast, its wisdom strong.
I laugh at the mirror, the grin of a clown,
Each moment's a jewel, no time to frown!

A rhapsody plays as I kick off my shoes,
With laughter and cheer, it's all I can choose.
So here's to the day, with humor as flight,
In this wacky world, everything feels right!

www.ingramcontent.com/pod-product-compliance
Lightning Source LLC
Chambersburg PA
CBHW071843160426
43209CB00003B/393